Nightmare

John Lowe

A Lowe Publication™

Text © John Lowe, 2011.

The right of John Lowe to be identified as author of this work has been asserted by him in accordance with the Copyright, Designs and Patents Act 1988.

All rights reserved. No part of this publication may be reproduced or transmitted in any form or by any means, electronic or mechanical, including photocopy, recording or any information storage and retrieval system, without permission in writing from the publisher.

Published in 2011 by:

**Lowe Publications
Linen Hall, 162 Regent Street
London, W1B 5TG
United Kingdom**

ISBN: 978-1-907824-05-0

Layout and illustrations by Giorgio Giussani.

Edited by Judi Hunter.

Printed in London by Empress Litho Ltd.

I have devised a unique template for interview preparation. It redefines an interview as 'an opportunity to perform rather than a situation to be tested'. I use it for all my candidates and at all levels. It works. Feedback – 100% complementary.

Contents

About the author	8
Your interview profile	10
What is an interview?	12
Your Interview Profiler	14
Your strengths	16
Compiling Your Interview Profiler	18
Using Your Interview Profiler in the interview	24
The flipside – the interviewer	30
Conclusion	38
Your Interview Profiler – template	39

About the author

John Lowe, founding director of Regent Selection, Regent Coaching and Regent eLearning, is the author of *Your Lowe Profile* and one of the leading experts on career and personal development coaching.

John is a successful headhunter, recruitment consultant and coach and it is this rare combination of skills and his experience of having conducted over 20,000 interviews – all factors which collectively give him unique market and people insight. He personally coaches MBA students, university professors, Board directors and an extensive range of business executives.

The coaching always has a strong employability focus and John's first-hand knowledge of the market place is based on his expertise of conducting assignments with the world's largest corporations, SMEs and start-ups. Each industry and employment activity has its own dynamic and the structure and content of the coaching has been designed to embrace this divergence and variety. John has introduced an exciting new approach to conventional coaching through the identification and development of four distinct personality types. As the candidate recognises their type and individual strengths, they can then apply this knowledge to the critical employment stages of knowing what is their ideal job role, always successfully performing on interview and consistently enhancing a top performance at work. All these critical factors are described in the publication *Your Lowe Profile* which can be used as an expert career coaching reference.

On a personal note, John is a graduate of the University of London where his Masters in Philosophy had a particularly contemporary focus on the role of ethics in our changing workplace.

This booklet capitalises on John's vast experience of preparing candidates for interview. The Interview Profiler is different and encourages you to examine the process from a completely new perspective.

Your interview profile

This is an exciting subject to write about. The point of an interview is to get the job. A really good performance on interview will result in a job offer. Your whole life changes. You text friends, leave messages and send e-mails. You want to share the good news with everyone. It is amazing to think of the changes a new job brings to your lifestyle: new motivation, new journeys to make, new colleagues to meet, and a new financial perspective.

Your sole objective of an interview then is to be in a position of choice – to be offered the role.

This chapter will demonstrate how you can dramatically increase your chances of being offered the job. Interview preparation is core to our highly-successful reputation as recruiters nationally and internationally. Its innovative approach challenges conventional advice. Its new, fresh approach redefines the interview. Your positive, successful performance will create a positive, successful outcome.

I have prepared many thousands of candidates for interviews and this is one of my particular specialisms. I have developed an interview format based on a unique combination of experience as a career coach, recruitment consultant and headhunter. I visit clients, find out their needs and relay that information to candidates. Whilst each role and candidate is unique, I have developed an **Interview Profiler**, which ensures that candidates present themselves confidently, positively and articulately. My research is uniquely based on over 20,000 face-to-face interviews.

What is an interview?

Most candidates envisage an interview primarily as a test or examination. In terms of feedback, it is not uncommon for a candidate to be asked by a friend, 'How well did you do?' and the answer to be, 'I think I did well. I think I answered all the questions,' or 'I don't know. I was not able to answer some questions'. In this instance, the interview was viewed as a knowledge-based exercise, a question and answer scenario rather like a quiz – the more questions you answer correctly the better you are judged.

Importantly, and right at the outset, we need to redefine the role of an interview. Contrary to what you might envisage, an interview is an opportunity to perform rather than simply to be tested.

As a candidate, it can be difficult to know what preparations to make for an interview as there are so many aspects of the event that are unpredictable.

- *How do I break the ice?*
- *Should I try and establish a rapport with the interviewer?*
- *What sort of person is the interviewer?*
- *Are they quiet, shy, friendly or aggressive?*
- *What mood will they be in?*
- *I want to come across as positive and confident, but not arrogant and pompous – how do I balance those factors in my presentation?*
- *I don't think I know enough about the job! I hope they don't ask me too many questions.*
- *I have looked at the website, but it does not help much in terms of this role.*
- *If there is an interview panel, which person should be the focus of my answers?*

Your Interview Profiler

The interview tool, **Your Interview Profiler**, is designed to ensure that candidates give the most positive and articulate account of their skills. It changes the emphasis from a question/answer interaction to the interviewee making a presentation about their relevant skills and creating a positive profile.

The challenge I had was the following: I was sending candidates for interview throughout the world to Bahrain, Paris, London, Geneva, Barbados, Lagos, Munich, Burkina Faso, Rotterdam and Düsseldorf. My contact with these clients was only by telephone and I could not brief my candidates as to their personalities and interview styles.

The candidate cannot properly prepare for a situation where the parameters are unknown. However, what the candidate can do is prepare and present a powerful synopsis of their skills that would impress any audience. Integrate this format into interview dialogue and interaction and you will see at first hand the benefit, relevance and power of Your Interview Profiler.

As a recruitment consultant, I use this method to prepare all my candidates for client interviews. As a career coach, I use this profiler to instruct all my clients in the art of interview preparation – senior executives on external interview or internal appraisal, MBA students returning to India, China, Africa and Europe. It works for panel interviews and it works when you have multiple interviews for different jobs and are wondering how to adjust your style to each interview. It works cross-culturally. It is not country specific, it is not role specific. It is always **you** specific.

Your strengths

As a prelude to developing a powerful presentation of your personality, you must answer the question:

What are my particular strengths and how have they worked for me in the past?

A key output of this process is the identification of your four most character defining and commercially relevant strengths, and the subsequent creation of Your Interview Profiler that directs you to align each of these strengths with two brief, descriptive and, where possible, quantifiable examples of how they have manifested themselves in your working life to date.

Your choice of strengths will depend on the circumstances in which you are applying them.

If you are preparing for a general interview or one where you are not clear about the job requirements, then choose the four strengths that generally best describe your personality.

If you are aware of the job description and have a clear understanding of the soft skills required, then you should choose and elaborate on those particular skills that are most relevant to the job. For example, if you are preparing for a sales type role, then goal orientated, persuasive, good communicator and decisive would be complementary and focused choices of strengths.

If you are preparing for a technical interview involving IT, accounting or banking, then analytical, organised, good under pressure and works independently might be personality characteristics that would naturally complement this type of work environment.

Compiling Your Interview Profiler

This is always a motivational and exciting journey of self-discovery. This is all about you, your strengths, your achievements. This is a time for you to evaluate and reflect on your achievements and your unique balance of personality (soft skills) and your experience to date, both academic and work (technical skills). Start the evaluation process and discover what unique talents and experiences you have to offer your next employer.

So let's recap. Your Interview Profiler is a template featuring four of your personality characteristics. Each characteristic is supported, confirmed and endorsed by two examples from your CV.

Your Interview Profiler

To illustrate its utility, an example of Your Interview Profiler has been compiled below for a Creative Manager on interview for a Design Manager's role.

1st strength:

Communication

a) Presentations:

In my current role, I make presentations to Directors of large advertising agencies and to Senior Executives within FMCG multiples.

b) Creative:

My own department of 26 staff comprises designers and highly-commercial staff, and I successfully get the disparate teams together to work effectively and collaboratively.

2nd strength:

Creative

a) New designs:

I have been responsible for product and packaging designs that have been accepted by the client in a project worth £5 million.

b) Run studio:

I manage a studio of 7 designers, which means training, mentoring and promoting new creative ideas and design skills.

3rd strength:

Commercial

a) Keep to budgets:

I am involved in the formulation of my department's budget with the main Board. In the last 3 years I have never exceeded the budget.

b) Increased profit by 10%:

I have also consistently increased profits, frequently exceeding the target by over 10%.

4th strength:

> **Organised**
>
> a) **Manage projects:**
>
> I currently manage 10 different projects ranging in value from £300k to £7 million. Good organisation and a highly-structured approach to critical path management for all projects, which have separate timescales and content, is vital for successful execution and delivery.
>
> b) **Part-time MA:**
>
> Two years ago I completed an MA whilst working full time. Successfully managing the priorities was vital.

Your Interview Profiler adds an extra dimension to the interview structure and ensures that you create a positive, powerful impression. Thus, dramatically increasing your chances of being offered the role.

Let me give you an example:

If I were developing my own Interview Profiler, I might choose Communicator as one of my strengths and use the following two endorsements:

I believe I have strong communication skills as I must engage with Senior Directors across many industries and activities such as oil, finance, retail and IT. Each activity has a different dynamic and culture.

I also coach MBA full-time cohorts from leading universities. Each cohort will have at least 15 different nationalities. This cultural mix means I must communicate and coach in sympathy with the student's culture and personality. I have received over 95 per cent positive feedback.

I have chosen Communicator as a dominant skill choice and endorsed the skill with two real examples. Replicate this format four times, and you will have developed a powerful and relevant Interview Profiler.

Your Interview Profiler provides you with a hard-wired framework on which to focus the discussion of your traits and past experiences during interviews. You will feel more confident, speak with more clarity and do yourself full justice at interview, having familiarised yourself with and internalised Your Interview Profiler prior to interview. Your performance will be more competent, confident and successful and you will no longer leave an interview with the feeling that you might have neglected to mention any unique selling points.

You will no longer feel: 'I am not sure how I got on'; 'I'm not sure if I answered the questions correctly'; 'I am not really sure what they were looking for'. Rather, you will be sure: 'I did my best. I presented myself positively and supported my points. My presentation was well prepared.'

You have now developed a presentation about your dominant skills and given examples of how you achieved and practised these skills. Practise delivering this as you would a public speech. It works. It gives you a structure to present yourself to your potential employer.

The interviewer can only make a judgement based on what you say and how you say it. Be proactive. Sitting quietly waiting for a question is too passive and will not give you the opportunity to perform positively.

Using Your Interview Profiler in the interview

You can now use Your Interview Profiler to perform at your best on interview. For example:

Question:

How do you think you will cope with aggressive clients?

Answer:

I believe I am a strong communicator. When I worked in customer support, there were complaints from dissatisfied customers. I received the highest number of compliments from clients for dealing with their problems. When I was leading the debating team at university, the environment was competitive and aggressive. I coached our team to deal with truculent behaviours and how to use humour to deflate a contentious argument. So I believe I have the skills to deal effectively with difficult clients.

Traditionally, interviews are conducted on an

autobiographic basis from the interviewee's perspective. In other words, you give a synopsis on what you have done, where you have worked and what you have achieved.

To adopt Your Interview Profiler method requires a radical rethink on the optimum format for interviews. In contrast to the autobiographic style, this method concentrates on you, in other words, your personality. This benefits you by allowing you to articulate your strengths and it benefits the employer as it provides a more useful and transparent means of assessing your suitability.

Remember, from an employer's perspective, the candidate is being assessed for a role that will be new to them involving new challenges, new situations, new cultures and it is the candidate's positive personality characteristics and how they articulate them that will determine their success, rather than the fact that they have fulfilled a similar role in the past.

Using Your Interview Profiler, which highlights your personality characteristics and endorses each characteristic by examples from your previous performance, must therefore constitute the most powerful interview presentation style.

Clearly, we have to talk about the past (autobiographic), but we lead with our personality characteristics and use our past as a means by which we can endorse our strengths.

The amazing fact about Your Interview Profiler is its simplicity, adaptability and success record. It will dramatically increase your chances of being offered the role.

You can use four characteristics that you think best describe your personality. Or you can vary your choice to adapt to a particular job interview. There is no right or wrong choice. Only use those characteristics that best describe your strengths and which you can endorse by example.

When you are being interviewed, it is normal for the interviewer to volunteer information such as a synopsis of the company and details about the job, its duties and responsibilities. Using Your Interview Profiler you are volunteering details about yourself so that the interviewer can make a judgement and compare you and the job. Your Interview Profiler has an outstanding success record.

The most difficult question you could be asked on interview is: 'Tell me about your personality.' This verbally bowls most people out and leads to one or two fairly sparse monosyllabic statements. This reaction is totally understandable, though logically it is a question we should be expert at answering. Our personality is something we rarely talk about or describe in isolation. Yet, we must identify and talk about it as personality traits and strengths are fundamental to our success at work. The sequence of formatting, adopting and presenting Your Interview Profiler is challenging to describe. Ideally, it requires one-to-one coaching sessions and hence I have used different scenarios to ensure you grasp the fundamentals.

I shall conclude my description with the following challenge:

Practice:

> *You are one of 10 candidates who must give a 30-minute presentation about yourself to a panel of three interviewers. You are not briefed about the role and your presentation will be interrupted by questions from the panel.*
>
> *To prepare for this challenge, you must focus on your personality, your experience and give examples of why you think you have a successful track record to date. This emphasis on you as the prime focus, rather than the role, is the fundamental strength and success of Your Interview Profiler.*

This advanced format supersedes the more traditional autobiographic descriptive-based style whereby you simply describe chronologically your past experiences. Adopt Your Interview Profiler and you will dramatically increase your success ratio of interview to job offers.

The flip side – the interviewer

I believe that the success of my coaching is the fact that the focus is always from the employer's perspective, which means that your preparation and presentations are always impactive, relevant and targeted. The more you can know about the interviewer's role and envisage the interview from their 'side of the table', the more enhanced your understanding of what constitutes an excellent performance will be. The flip side will help you to better understand the power of Your Interview Profiler as an exciting interview tool.

If interviewing is something you do not like and feel that you are not particularly good at, then that is a positive or realistic frame of mind on which to build and improve your technique.

If interviewing is something you believe you are good at and 'I have interviewed lots of people' is your typical suppositional reaction, then you may need coaching in conducting one-to-one assessments. This type of positive reaction can mirror-image an arrogant attitude that portrays a negative learning disposition summarised as, 'I know people. I can sum people up.'

There are three major criteria that influence recruitment interviewing:

1 The personality characteristics of the interviewer.
2 The environment and process.
3 The details of the role.

Interviewing is never a simple exercise of 'summing people up'. It is an exercise in assessing a candidate against the benchmark of a job role. It is circumstantial, situational and contextual. The interviewer is identifying the soft and technical skills of the role and matching these to the candidate. Whilst the interviewer is endeavouring to be as fair and objective as possible, it can be a difficult exercise and depends on the personality type of the interviewer.

The publication *Your Lowe Profile* describes the four dominant personality types and their behaviours – the Supporter, the Influencer, the Creative and the Analyst. You can refer to this book if it is important to advance your interviewing skills. Both the Supporter and Influencer have a strong people focus, with the Supporter emphasising their helping and caring personality strengths. The Influencer enjoys selling and the commercial challenge it presents. The Creative and Analyst are predominantly task focused and their interview styles will manifest this dominant trait.

The Supporter will tend to concentrate on soft skills, endeavouring to establish a rapport with the candidate and judging them on emotional criteria – 'I like/dislike' basis. To improve their skills, they should concentrate on the technical aspects of the role and depersonalise the content of the questions posed.

The Influencer must focus on listening. They will have a tendency to talk too much and therefore not give the interviewee a fair opportunity to ask as well as answer questions. Interviewing is a two-way dialogue, not an interrogation, where both parties can assess each other. When explaining or elaborating on points of the job description, the Influencer should be brief and not offer a verbal dissertation. They must try not to put too much 'self' into the interview.

The Creative and Analyst normally adopt a balanced interactive interview style. They focus on the technical responsibilities and can dispassionately assess a candidate's objectives. Today's employment environment is predominantly task over people focused and, therefore, this objective approach replicates today's best interviewing techniques.

These scenarios emphasise the benefits of knowing your personality type and applying it to an interview situation.

- *First impressions are everything.*
- *I can tell after two minutes whether the candidate is right for the role.*
- *It's important to break the ice and chat informally and put the candidate at their ease.*

These views, I am afraid, are not the observations of experienced interviewers and mean that the interviewer is judging from a narrow perspective. The fact that a mathematical modeller presents themselves as a taciturn, verbally reclusive, monosyllabic candidate can be a positive indicator if you are seeking a highly numerate and technical analyst, whilst the energetic, verbose, gregarious candidate may be an excellent fit for that business development role you are seeking to fill.

We know that each situation is very different and the determinants that will influence the outcome are varied. Nevertheless, there are some general pointers that I can recommend and which you can adopt whilst assessing candidates.

The past can tell the future

Regard historic performance and attitude as a replication and indication of future achievement. The saying, 'Actions speak louder than words' is true in this respect.

Yes, I did have a lot of time off because I did not find the job very interesting, but I like the sound of this role and I would be much more motivated.

This would not be regarded as a convincing answer.

Timekeeping is also a crucial indicator. If a candidate is late for interview, they will need a very good excuse. About 3 per cent of my candidates arrive late and most often, when I ask what time they set off, I discover that their time allocation was too intolerant and was based on the assumption that all modes of transport run perfectly on time, without signal failures or traffic jams. Most candidates allow a generous time tolerance for interviews. Successful applicants are rarely late.

A candidate's voluntary comments are much more valid and reflective of their personality and attitude than those generated by direct questions. You must create an environment and atmosphere where the candidate can make spontaneous comments. Ask open-ended questions that may be tangential to the main point and the candidate's answer will be a more authentic reflection of their personality. Having a very prescriptive list of fixed questions that mirror-image a 'question time' challenge will not allow you to discover the candidate's real interpersonal skills.

Generally speaking, the balance of conversation should be 70/30 in favour of the candidate. Do not conduct stress interviews unless you are highly experienced in managing the outcomes. You may read publications itemising the most difficult questions to be asked and suggesting classic answers. I do not follow this trend. My role as an interviewer is to ascertain if there is a match of skills and not to intimidate or browbeat the candidate with an aggressive inquisition.

In summation, keep the format transparent and adopt a listening style. Let the candidate volunteer their opinion. Identify the skills match and when the interview has ended adhere to your immediate decision. Do not feel that you have to justify your decision with pages of narrative. The brain replicates a powerful processing unit and your decision is therefore informed not spontaneous.

Interviewing is a learning process at which you become more competent and, through experience, progressively skilful.

You can refer to my descriptions of personality and behaviour type in *Your Lowe Profile*, which will help you to assess candidates more fairly and contextually. Don't expect the Analyst to be an excellent communicator nor the Influencer to be expert at quantitative analysis – neither is their forte.

Create a relaxed environment and ask real not posing questions and your assessment of the candidate, though subjective, will most often be accurate.

Conclusion

Introducing you to interviewing skills has added an extra dimension to your knowledge of interviews. You have been introduced to the skills required from the interviewer's perspective. This insight will help you to focus on a more defined target. You now know what the interviewer wants. You now know they are on your 'side of the desk'. They want to offer you the role and to ensure you do not disappoint them, complete Your Interview Profiler and prepare for your performance.

Your Interview Profiler

1st strength:

A)

B)

2nd strength:

A)

B)

Your Interview Profiler continued...

3rd strength:

A)

B)

4th strength:

A)

B)